In the Garden

Comparing Numbers

Jane Gould

Consultants

Chandra C. Prough, M.S.Ed.
National Board Certified
Newport-Mesa
  Unified School District

Jodene Smith, M.A.
ABC Unified School District

Publishing Credits

Dona Herweck Rice, *Editor-in-Chief*
Lee Aucoin, *Creative Director*
Chris McIntyre, M.A.Ed., *Editorial Director*
James Anderson, M.S.Ed., *Editor*
Aubrie Nielsen, M.S.Ed., *Associate Education Editor*
Neri Garcia, *Senior Designer*
Stephanie Reid, *Photo Editor*
Rachelle Cracchiolo, M.S.Ed., *Publisher*

Image Credits

p.12 craftvision/iStockphoto; p.17 Vasyl Helevachuk/Dreamstime; All other images: Shutterstock

Teacher Created Materials

5301 Oceanus Drive
Huntington Beach, CA 92649-1030
http://www.tcmpub.com
ISBN 978-1-4333-3431-3
© 2012 Teacher Created Materials, Inc.
BP 5028

Table of Contents

In the Garden 4

You Try It! 24

Solve the Problem 28

Glossary 30

Answer Key 32

How many?

2 bees

How many?

4 flies
4 is **greater** than 2.

How many?

4 apples

How many?

5 oranges
5 is greater than 4.

How many?

2 rabbits

How many?

8 beetles
8 is greater than 2.

How many?

3 pea pods

How many?

2 ears of corn
2 is **less** than 3.

How many?

6 ladybugs

How many?

3 snails
3 is less than 6.

How many?

10 carrots

How many?

5 tomatoes
5 is less than 10.

How many?

3 grasshoppers

How many?

3 worms
3 is **equal** to 3.

How many?

7 tulips

How many?

7 roses
7 is equal to 7.

How many?

9 moths

How many?

9 ants
9 is equal to 9.

There are **more** ladybugs than ants.

4

2

There are less rabbits than birds.

5

6

There are equal moths and lizards.

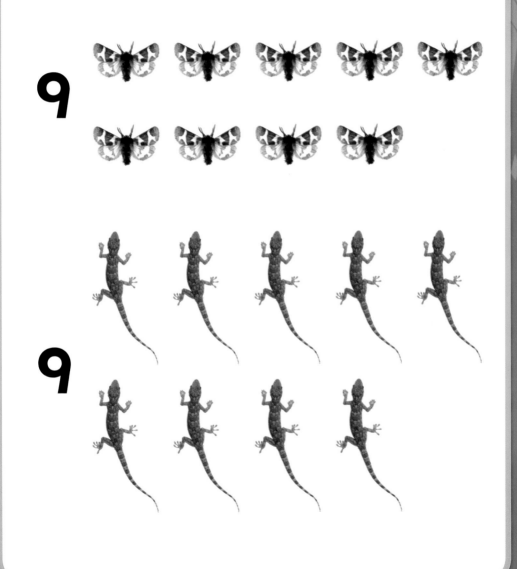

9

9

Count the bees.
Count the spiders.

Are there more bees
or spiders?

How many butterflies are there?

1. Point to the group that has an equal amount.

2. Point to the group that has less.

3. Point to the group that has more.

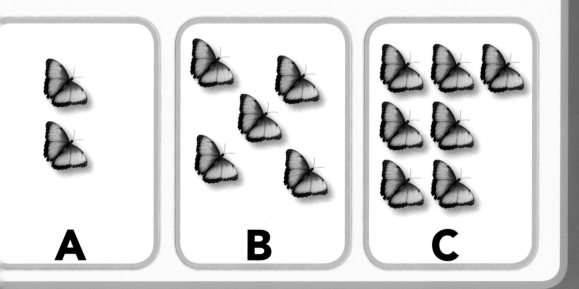

A B C

Who has more?
Who has less?

Materials
- ✓ number cards 0–10
- ✓ blocks

1 Work with a friend.

2 Pick a number card.

3 Count out the number of blocks and stack them.

4 Who has more blocks? Who has less?

Glossary

equal—the same amount

greater—a larger amount

less—a smaller
number or amount

more—a larger
number or amount

ANSWER KEY

You Try It!

Page 24:
5 bees; 2 spiders

Page 25:
There are more bees than spiders.

Page 26:
5 butterflies

Page 27:
1. B

2. A

3. C

Solve the Problem
Answers will vary.